Food Dudes

SAM J. PORCELLO

Oreo Innovator

Heather C. Hudak

Checkerboard
Library

An Imprint of Abdo Publishing
www.abdopublishing.com

abdopublishing.com

Published by Abdo Publishing, a division of ABDO, PO Box 398166, Minneapolis, Minnesota 55439. Copyright © 2018 by Abdo Consulting Group, Inc. International copyrights reserved in all countries. No part of this book may be reproduced in any form without written permission from the publisher. Checkerboard Library™ is a trademark and logo of Abdo Publishing.

Printed in the United States of America, North Mankato, Minnesota
062017
092017

THIS BOOK CONTAINS
RECYCLED MATERIALS

Production: Mighty Media, Inc.
Editor: Rebecca Felix
Cover Photographs: Courtesy the Porcello family (inset), iStockphoto (main)
Interior Photographs: Alamy, p. 9; AP Images, p. 27; Courtesy the Porcello family, pp. 1, 5, 11, 15, 17, 21, 23, 25; iStockphoto, p. 24; Mike Mozart/Flickr, p. 19; Shutterstock, pp. 4, 7, 8, 13

Publisher's Cataloging-in-Publication Data

Names: Hudak, Heather C., 1975-, author.
Title: Sam J. Porcello: Oreo innovator / by Heather C. Hudak.
Other titles: Oreo innovator
Description: Minneapolis, MN : Abdo Publishing, 2018. | Series: Food dudes |
    Includes bibliographical references and index.
Identifiers: LCCN 2016962531 | ISBN 9781532110849 (lib. bdg.) |
    ISBN 9781680788693 (ebook)
Subjects: LCSH: Porcello, Sam J., 1935-2012--Juvenile literature. | Nabisco
    (Firm)--United States--Biography--Juvenile literature. | Inventor--United
    States--Biography--Juvenile literature. | Scientist--United States--Biography--
    Juvenile literature.
Classification: DDC 641.6 [B]--dc23
LC record available at http://lccn.loc.gov/2016962531

Contents

Early Life

Some people believe the way a person eats an Oreo reveals aspects about his or her personality!

How do you eat your Oreo cookies? Do you dunk them in milk? Or maybe you twist off the top and eat the **crème** filling first! You might be surprised to learn that the man who invented the creamy center did not like to eat sweets. But that did not stop Sam

Sam with his mother, Theresa

J. Porcello from creating the famous filling inside Oreos, as well as many other sweet treats.

Samuel Joseph Porcello was born in May 1935 in Newark, New Jersey. He went by Sam. Sam's mother's name was Theresa. Little is known about Sam's father. Sam was raised by his mother and his stepfather, Jerry Porcello, who legally adopted Sam.

Sam was an only child, but he was part of a huge extended family. His mother was the oldest of 15 children. Many of her brothers and sisters were close in age to Sam. Sam's uncle Ralph was only two years older than him. The two boys were very good friends. Sam felt more like a brother to many of his mother's **siblings** than he did their nephew.

Sam was also very close to his mother. She loved Sam very much and **doted** on him. There was almost nothing Theresa would not do for Sam. She even ironed his socks and underwear!

Education Matters

As a child, Sam spent a great deal of time with his grandmother, Esterina Mazzuca. Esterina was often in the kitchen, cooking for her family. Sam sometimes helped her. Soon he took an interest in cooking too.

Sam went to Barringer High School in Newark. After graduation, he spent one year studying at nearby Seton Hall University. He went on to earn a bachelor's degree in **chemistry** from Fairleigh Dickinson University in Teaneck, New Jersey.

Porcello worked hard to put himself through school. He often worked as many as three different jobs during the school year. After finishing university, Porcello took a job as a math teacher in 1959. But Porcello did not earn enough money to support himself. The next year, he set out to find a new job.

Porcello hoped to work at a **cosmetics** company creating new products. One company offered Porcello a job, and he planned to accept it. But before he could, the company learned Porcello was **colorblind**. If Porcello couldn't see colors, how could he make cosmetics? Porcello returned to his job search.

Newark, Sam's hometown, is very near Hoboken, New Jersey, where the first Oreos were sold in 1912.

Sweet Career Start

Porcello's job search didn't last long. In 1960, he was offered a position developing foods at Charms Candy Company. Charms made all kinds of candies. But the candy it was best known for was its lollipops.

But Porcello worked at Charms for only a short time. He soon took a new a job, as a food **chemist** with Nabisco food company. Porcello was told he could one day earn up to $12,000 per year working there. This was a huge increase from his Charms salary.

Nabisco, or the National Biscuit Company, formed in 1898. It made snack foods and bakery products. In 1912, Nabisco first introduced Oreo cookies.

Early Oreos were a bit different than the cookies we know today. The first Oreos were made from two chocolate cookies with either **vanilla** frosting or lemon **meringue** in the center. The vanilla cookies were much more popular, so Nabisco stopped making the lemon cookies in the 1920s.

By the time Porcello started working at Nabisco, Oreo cookies were quite popular. But that did not mean they could not be improved. So, Porcello got right to work.

Porcello worked in Nabisco's research and development department. Part of his role was to create new products or find ways to make old ones better. And that is just what he did.

OREO SANDWICH

CHOCOLATE FLAVORED WAFERS WITH CREAMY LEMON OR VANILLA FLAVORED FILLING

Oreos were invented 26 years before chocolate chip cookies!

Cookies & Change

Porcello worked mainly on cookies and crackers at Nabisco. He quickly started coming up with fresh ideas. One of them included a new way to make the **crème** filling for Oreo cookies.

Food science had come a long way between 1912 when Oreos **debuted** and the 1960s when Porcello began at Nabisco. Many new ingredients were being used, and cooking equipment had improved. Using these resources, Porcello began experimenting with the original Oreo filling recipe.

At the time, the filling was a type of sugar icing. It had a grainy **texture**. Porcello wanted to make it creamier. He started changing the fats and oils used to make the filling. Porcello led a team of food scientists and **chemists**. Together, they worked to make the Oreo filling even more **delicious**.

As Porcello's career at Nabisco got underway, his personal life saw big change too. It was around this time that friends introduced him to a woman named Karen. Porcello and Karen started dating in the late 1960s. They married soon after. In 1969, the couple had a son, David. The next year, they welcomed a second son, Curtis.

Karen and Sam with their oldest son, David (center)

Cocoa Connoisseur

Porcello continued to work hard at Nabisco. Improving the Oreo **crème** filling wasn't the only contribution he made to the cookie or to the company. Porcello was also very knowledgeable about all things chocolate.

While at Nabisco, Porcello became a cocoa **connoisseur**. Cocoa is the powder used to make chocolate. Porcello took specialized training classes to learn about cocoa. He also attended many chocolate **conventions** in the United States and Europe. Soon, Porcello was considered one of the world's leading cocoa experts.

Porcello was the first person Nabisco employees went to for advice about chocolate. Over time, he got to know so much about cocoa that Nabisco gave him a very important task. Porcello was to approve the quality of all cocoa shipments for the entire company.

Nabisco used a lot of cocoa to make its sweet treats. Some shipments contained thousands, or even millions, of pounds of cocoa. These large shipments arrived to Nabisco on trucks or trains. Porcello's job approving all that cocoa was a huge responsibility.

Nabisco uses about 18 million pounds (8.2 million kg) of cocoa in Oreo cookies each year.

One of the ways Porcello knew if cocoa was good or not was by its color. He would often turn down entire shipments because they were the wrong color. However, Porcello never told any of his cocoa suppliers he was **colorblind**. It did not make any difference what **hue** he saw when he looked at the cocoa. All that mattered was that Porcello knew it was not the color it should be.

Mr. Oreo

Porcello became known at Nabisco for his expertise on chocolate. But to his **colleagues**, he was most famous for his work on Oreos. In fact, many of them called Porcello "Mr. Oreo"!

Oreos were around before Porcello's time at Nabisco. But he made them the popular treat they are today. After perfecting Oreo's **crème** filling, Porcello worked on new variations of the cookie.

Several variations Porcello worked on experimented with the sizes of Oreos. Some were very tiny, only about the size of a penny. Others were as big as three inches (7.62 cm) across. This is nearly double the size of a regular Oreo!

Porcello also sought ingredients to make special variations of Oreos. He loved to travel, and explored the globe looking for just the right ingredients to add to the cookie. In the 1980s, Porcello gave Oreos a new look when he covered them in white chocolate or chocolate fudge. He found the chocolate for the coating at a trade show in Europe.

Porcello also tested different flavors for Oreo's crème filling. This included crème flavored with **vanilla**, chocolate, coffee, and

Porcello (center) attends a meeting at Nabisco. He got along very well with his colleagues.

peppermint. He also worked on creating Double Stuf Oreos, which had twice as much filling as the original cookies.

Porcello would bring each new creation he tested home for his family to try. However, not every idea Mr. Oreo had made it to the shelves. Some did not make it past Nabisco's **rigorous** process for testing each new product.

Tough Test Kitchen

Nabisco had very strict standards for its foods. Before a new product went to **market**, it first had to pass a series of tests. Porcello's Oreo creations were no exception.

One type of test new Nabisco products were put through was a taste test. In a taste test, members of the public were asked to taste and then review the new food. Nabisco's marketing team would then use this feedback to help decide what new products to release.

Another Nabisco new-product test involved manufacturing. The new Oreos had to be made for eight straight hours without any major issues. The company wanted to make sure that no problems in production would occur once they invested in making a new food.

Employees could bake quite a lot of Oreos in eight hours! In fact, there were so many that Nabisco used huge trucks to collect them all off the manufacturing lines. The cookies were taken away and destroyed. The manufacturing method had not yet been **verified**. So, the test cookies could not be sold. They were often ground up and sent to farmers to use in pig feed.

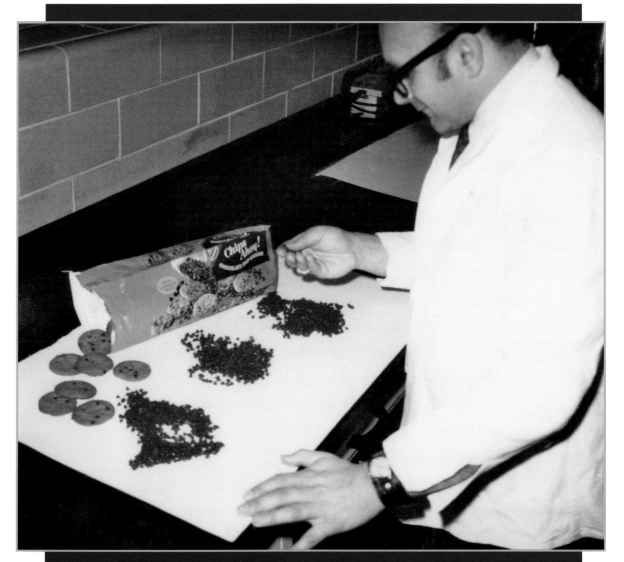

Porcello tests chocolate samples for Chips Ahoy! cookies in the Nabisco lab.

New Ideas

While not all of Porcello's cookie creations made it past Nabisco's test kitchen, many did. Porcello worked beyond recipe creation too. He, in partnership with other Nabisco scientists, also had a winning idea involving production. It was a way to quickly cool food products after they had been cooked.

Until then, food companies had to wait for foods to cool before they could be packaged. For some products, the process was **complex** and took a long time. This led to wasted money as paid employees had to spend work time waiting to complete an order.

Porcello and his **colleagues** found a way to lessen this cooling time using a corona current. This is an electrical current that was used to cool certain foods. This included foods with a liquid coating, such as cookies covered in chocolate.

Prior to using this method, foods with a liquid coating required a very particular cooling process. This was to ensure their outer layer was smooth and glossy and not cracked or discolored. This process began on conveyor belts and tunnels. Then, the product needed to sit in a cooler for an extended period of time.

Mallomars are one product quickly cooled to a glossy finish using Nabisco's patented process.

With the corona current, this extended cooling was eliminated. The method cooled these foods in such a way that they could be packaged right after the tunnel cooling process. This saved Nabisco a lot of time and money.

Porcello, along with the help of other inventors, patented the improved cooling method in 1974. This was the first of five patents Porcello was part of over the years. In the 1980s, he also helped invent four patented recipes. They were for special fillers and creams. The patents protected the recipes from being stolen by other companies.

Special Honors

By the 1980s, Porcello had worked on many different food products for Nabisco. These included the cookies Chips Ahoy! and Fig Newtons, today called simply Newtons. He also worked on Ritz and SnackWell's crackers. With all these foods, Porcello either helped create them or improved recipes to make them better. But he was best known for his continual work on Oreos.

The company recognized Porcello's devotion to making Nabisco products the best they could be. In 1986, it held a gala to celebrate the Oreo's seventy-fifth birthday. The gala took place at the historic hotel the Waldorf Astoria New York. The hotel is thought to be one of the nicest places in the world to stay or host an event. But the location was just one reason this gala was special. Another reason was that Porcello was made a guest of honor at the event.

Three years later, Nabisco again honored Porcello's work, naming him a principal scientist of the company. A Nabisco principal scientist only earns this honorary title through coworker recommendations. This meant only those employees whom several **colleagues** believed to be outstanding were nominated.

Once coworkers nominate a principal scientist, the Nabisco management team does a thorough review of that employee. They determine if he or she has earned the title. In Porcello's case, Nabisco decided he most certainly had! Porcello added principal scientist to his list of roles at Nabisco, which included program director of research and development.

In 1993, Porcello retired from Nabisco. His work forever changed the face of the Oreo cookie. Now it was time for Porcello to take on new adventures.

Porcello worked at Nabisco for nearly half his life!

Life After Oreo

Porcello had retired from Nabisco, but he kept in contact with several former **colleagues** there. The company also kept in contact with Porcello. Nabisco held annual dinners for retirees, and Porcello often attended.

Retirement hadn't meant the end of Porcello's ties to Nabisco. It also didn't mean Porcello was ready to stop working. The same year he retired, he started his own business consulting for other food companies. One of them was Fleetwood Snacks. This company makes cookies and crackers to sell in convenience stores and vending machines. Porcello's new business was very successful.

Food companies weren't the only organizations to benefit from Porcello's new consulting work. He also volunteered with non-profit organization ACDI/VOCA. It helps developing countries around the world build their economies.

Porcello remained involved with ACDI/VOCA for many years. Around 2008, the organization sent Porcello to Thailand. There, he used his expert knowledge of the food industry to help a local company develop nut-based products.

Porcello enjoyed watching sports during his retirement. He especially liked football.

Family Man

Porcello's volunteer and consulting work involved a lot of travel. He enjoyed traveling so much that he often did so in his free time too. Porcello loved spending time at the beach. One of his favorite places to travel to was Sanibel Island in Florida.

Many of the beaches on Sanibel Island are nearly covered with seashells.

A favorite hobby also drew Porcello to the beach. He loved sailing and worked with the US Coast Guard Auxiliary Flotilla 16-05. This organization is made up of **civilians** who help support US Coast Guard missions. Porcello was a courtesy marine examination officer. He checked boats to make sure they met safety standards.

When not traveling to the beach, Porcello also often traveled to Las Vegas, Nevada, to visit his son David. Family was important to

Porcello. He loved spending time with his wife, children, and two grandchildren, Jacqueline and Curtis Jr. Porcello's dog, Evry, was also an important part of the family.

Evry was a papillon named after a city in France that Porcello had once visited. Porcello was 71 when he adopted Evry. It was his first, and only, dog. The two were inseparable for the remainder of Porcello's life.

Porcello relaxes at his family beach house.

Living Legacy

Porcello became an important figure in Nabisco history. He died on May 12, 2012, but his memory lives on in the many products he worked on at the company. From SnackWell's to Ritz, Porcello was the brains behind some of the best-known snack foods ever made. But his greatest contribution there was to the Oreo cookie.

Today, Oreos are considered to be the best-selling cookie of all time. They are sold in more than 100 countries. The classic, white **crème** filling is still a favorite of many people. But several special variations of the filling have since been created. This includes peanut butter, key lime pie, birthday cake frosting, and even candy corn!

The cookies containing the filling have also undergone changes in recent years. They are offered in as many wild flavors as the crème filing. They have also changed in size. But no matter the flavor or size, all Oreos are stuffed with a filling based on the recipe Porcello patented.

Porcello helped make many of Nabisco's foods what they are today. So, next time you twist open an Oreo, remember Porcello and his successful science lab creation. Then, dunk it milk!

People around the world eat more than 20 million Oreos each day!

Timeline

1912	Nabisco first introduced Oreo cookies.
1935	Samuel Joseph Porcello was born in Newark, New Jersey.
1959	Porcello took a job as a math teacher.
1969	Porcello's wife, Karen, gave birth to the couple's first child, David.
1970	Porcello and Karen welcomed a second son, Curtis.
1974	Porcello, along with other Nabisco scientists, got his first patent.
1986	Porcello was the guest of honor at a gala celebrating the Oreo's seventy-fifth birthday.
1990	Nabisco gave Porcello the title principal scientist.
1993	Porcello retired from Nabisco.
2012	Porcello died on May 12.

What's in a Name?

No one knows for sure where the name Oreo comes from. Here are a few theories. Which one do you think is most likely? What other reasons can you think of to explain why the cookies were given the name Oreo?

The first Oreo cookies were said to be shaped like a baseball pitcher's mound or hill. *Oreo* is a Greek word that means "hill" or "mountain."

Originally, the cookies came in a gold package. In French, the word *or* means "gold."

A man claimed he came up with the word Oreo as part of a contest Nabisco held in the 1920s to find a name for the cookies. Nabisco, however, has said there was no such contest.

Glossary

chemistry - a science that focuses on substances and the changes they go through. A person who studies chemistry is a chemist.

civilian - a person who is not an active member of the military.

colleague - someone who works with others in a certain field, at a job, or on a particular project.

colorblind - unable to tell certain colors apart.

complex - having many parts, details, ideas, or functions.

connoisseur - a person who knows a lot about a subject, particularly how to recognize good quality in objects connected with that subject.

convention - a group of people meeting for a special purpose.

cosmetics - beauty products, especially makeup.

crème - cream or a substance with a thick, creamy consistency.

debut - to officially introduce a first appearance.

delicious - tasting or smelling very good.

dote - to pay someone a lot of attention, or show him or her a lot of fondness.

hue - a color or a shade of a color.

market - to advertise or promote an item for sale. This process is called marketing.

meringue - a dessert topping consisting of a baked mixture of stiffly beaten egg whites and sugar.

rigorous - strict and demanding, or done carefully and with a lot of attention to detail.

sibling - a brother or a sister.

texture (TEHKS-chuhr) - the look and feel of something.

vanilla - a flavoring made from the seed pods of a tropical orchid and used in several foods, especially sweets.

verified - confirmed as correct, accurate, or real.

Websites

To learn more about Food Dudes,
visit **abdobooklinks.com**. These links are routinely monitored
and updated to provide the most current information available.

Index